Powerful Queens

Written by Fiona Tomlinson

Collins

Did you know that some of the most fascinating rulers in history were female? Some queens were peaceful and some were great fighters. They ruled with intelligence and skill.

Queen Hatshepsut

Queen Boudicca

Here's an introduction to four powerful queens from history!

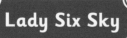

Lady Six Sky

Queen Elizabeth I

Queen Hatshepsut

Queen Hatshepsut was an ancient Egyptian ruler. She lived around 3500 years ago. Her **reign** lasted 20 years, and it was peaceful and successful.

Hatshepsut constructed many monuments.
These included a massive temple and a huge **obelisk**,
which still stands today.

Hapshetsut's obelisk

Hatshepsut reigned longest of all Egyptian queens.
Unlike many rulers, she had no ambition to **conquer**
far-off lands. She wanted to make Egypt rich and peaceful.

Hatshepsut sent people on expeditions to trade with other kingdoms. They returned with gold and luxury goods like **frankincense**.

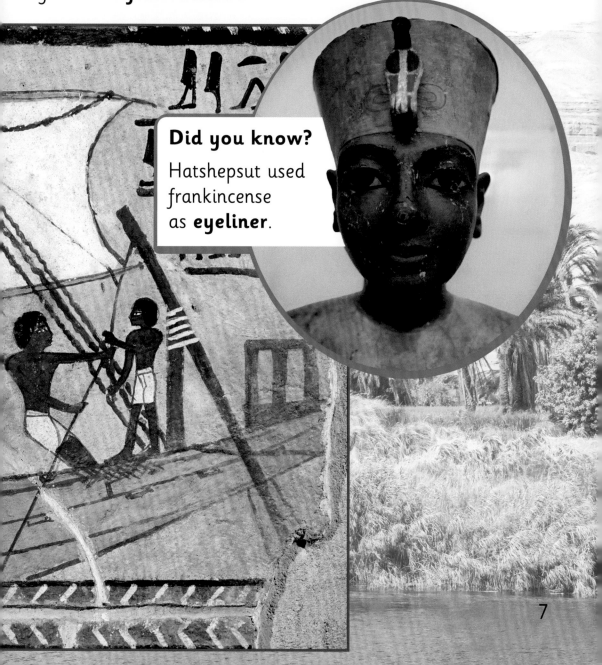

Did you know?

Hatshepsut used frankincense as **eyeliner**.

Queen Boudicca

Boudicca was an ancient Briton.
She was the queen of a tribe
and ruled nearly 2000 years ago.

Boudicca became ruler after her husband died. She battled against the Romans who had conquered her land.

Did you know?
The name Boudicca means victory!

Boudicca was on a mission to destroy the Romans' power.
Her army burnt and wrecked several Roman cities.

In the end, the Romans defeated Boudicca. No one knows how she died, but many believe she poisoned herself to avoid **capture**.

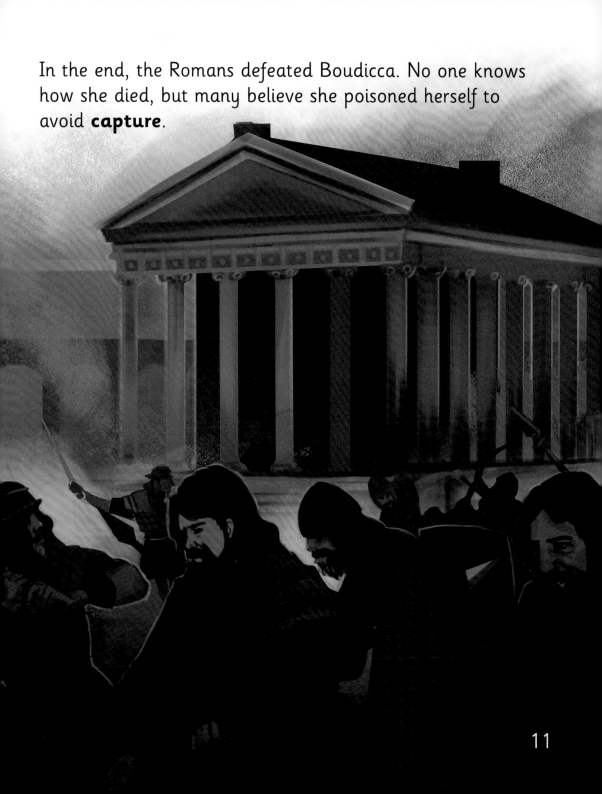

Lady Six Sky

Lady Six Sky lived in a **city-state** in Central America, over 1200 years ago.

She was sent on a mission to another city-state, to become its ruler and stop the city-states fighting each other.

It was unusual then to have a female ruler, but Lady Six Sky showed a lot of power and **aggression**.

Lady Six Sky won many battles. In one stone carving, she is shown standing on an enemy.

Queen Elizabeth I

Queen Elizabeth I lived over 400 years ago. When she came to the throne the **nation** was divided. People said that she would not be queen for long, but she reigned for 44 years!

Elizabeth showed that she could be strong and make peace. She had to fight the Spanish king and Scottish queen who wanted to take her throne.

Queen Elizabeth's reign was a time of exploration. She **knighted** Francis Drake after his **circumnavigation** of the world.

Drake was a well-known explorer.

Elizabeth had a good education and loved the **arts**. The **playwright** Shakespeare wrote many plays during her reign.

Did you know?

Queen Elizabeth could speak Welsh, Greek and Latin!

Glossary

aggression violence

arts books, music, plays, painting etc.

capture being taken prisoner

circumnavigation sailing all the way round the world

city-state a city that lives by its own rules

conquer take over by force

eyeliner eye make-up

frankincense a perfume that comes from a tree

knighted gave the title of knight or "Sir"

nation a land or country

obelisk a tall pillar made from stone

playwright someone who writes plays

reign the time when a king or queen ruled

Four powerful queens

Queen Hatshepsut

Queen Boudicca

1500 BCE   1000 BCE   500 BCE   0

Lady Six Sky

Queen Elizabeth I

500 CE   1000 CE   1500 CE   2000 CE

After reading

Letters and Sounds: Phases 5–6

Word count: 508

Focus phonemes: /s/ ce, c, sc /n/ kn, gn /sh/ ti, ci, ssi /c/ qu /r/ wr /zh/ s

Common exception words: of, to, the, said, were, one, people, today, great, many, who, eye, their

Curriculum links: History

National Curriculum learning objectives: Reading/word reading: apply phonic knowledge and skills as the route to decode words; read accurately by blending the sounds in words that contain the graphemes taught so far, especially recognising alternative sounds for graphemes; read accurately words of two or more syllables that contain the same graphemes as above; Reading/comprehension: understand both the books that they can already read accurately and fluently and those they listen to by: checking that the text makes sense to them as they read and correcting inaccurate reading, answering and asking questions

Developing fluency

- Your child may enjoy hearing you read the book.
- Take turns to read a page of the main text, encouraging them to read with expression, and not to miss reading the **Did you know?** boxes, and the captions.

Phonic practice

- Ask your child to read the following and identify the spellings of any /s/ sounds:

  city (*c*)   fascinating (*sc*)   intelligence (*ce*)
- Challenge them to think of some more words where "c" has the /s/ sound (e.g. *face, lace, central*, etc.)

Extending vocabulary

- Point to **fascinating** on page 2, and ask your child to think of a word that means the opposite (e.g. *boring*).
- Ask your child to add -less to these words and discuss the meaning of the new word:

  care (*careless* – e.g. *not cautious, sloppy*)
  home (*homeless* – e.g. *having no home*)
  help (*helpless* – *not able to take care of yourself*)